PORTRAIT OF MY LOVER AS A HORSE

Poetry by Selima Hill

BOOKS

Saying Hello at the Station (Chatto & Windus, 1984)*

My Darling Camel (Chatto & Windus, 1988)*

The Accumulation of Small Acts of Kindness (Chatto & Windus, 1989)

A Little Book of Meat (Bloodaxe Books, 1993)

Trembling Hearts in the Bodies of Dogs: New & Selected Poems (Bloodaxe Books, 1994): includes work from titles asterisked above, the complete text of *The Accumulation of Small Acts of Kindness,* and a new collection, *Aeroplanes of the World*

Violet (Bloodaxe Books, 1997)

Bunny (Bloodaxe Books, 2001)

Portrait of My Lover as a Horse (Bloodaxe Books, 2002)

CASSETTE

The Poetry Quartets: 2 (The British Council/Bloodaxe Books, 1998) [with Fleur Adcock, Carol Ann Duffy & U.A. Fanthorpe]

Selima Hill

PORTRAIT
OF MY LOVER
AS A HORSE

BLOODAXE BOOKS

ISBN: 1 85224 600 6

First published 2002 by
Bloodaxe Books Ltd,
Highgreen,
Tarset,
Northumberland NE48 1RP.

www.bloodaxebooks.com
For further information about Bloodaxe titles
please visit our website or write to
the above address for a catalogue.

Bloodaxe Books Ltd acknowledges
the financial assistance of Northern Arts.

Cover printing by J. Thomson Colour Printers Ltd, Glasgow.

Printed in Great Britain by
Cromwell Press Ltd, Trowbridge, Wiltshire.

CONTENTS

ACKNOWLEDGEMENTS

Acknowledgements are due to the editors of the following publications in which some of these poems first appeared: *Foolscap, The Gift: new writing for the NHS* (Stride, 2002), *The Guardian, Mslexia, New Delta Review* (USA), *Poetry London, Poetry Review, Resurgence, The Rialto* and *Wicked Poems* (Bloomsbury, 2002). Others were broadcast on *The Poetry Proms* (BBC Radio 4) and on *Nowhere* (Channel 4) and one was published as a Poetry Library postcard (Royal Festival Hall).

Thanks are also due to Micky, Trudi and Fred Macgregor for letting us borrow James Joyce, as well as to JJ himself, and to William and Cynthia Morrison-Bell for allowing our horse into their house (and to George for his horse-placating carrots).

Portrait of My Lover as an Angel

Nothing, as you know, would please me more
than if you were to find yourself in Heaven
standing on a cloud with nothing on
being measured by a large saint.

Portrait of My Lover's Arm

Your arm across my breast
is like a doll
nobody wants to cuddle
because it's headless.

Portrait of My Lover as Ash

My face
is like a face made of lips
being adored by a helpless drift of ash.

Portrait of My Lover with a Bag of Sweets

Whenever you think
I think I need a lover,
stop yourself.
I don't.
I need sweets.

Portrait of My Lover as a Bar of Soap

What I said I want
are lots of parrots
trampling on my back
like polo ponies
while you, O Lord,
congeal in the bathroom,
meekly getting used to being soap.

Portrait of My Lover as a Bay

To me,
you're tiny,
like a normal bay
being remembered by the open sea
where everything is blue,
and blue fields
go up and down
and up and down
like sorrow.

Portrait of My Lover as a Beetle

The look you give me is the sort of look
a beetle, Lord,
might give a large saint
who bicycles past across God's golden cumuli
and accidentally squishes
the beetle's foot.

Portrait of My Lover as a Blanket

You wet me
like a blanket made of throat
I drag across the bathroom
like a tail.

Portrait of My Lover as a Bride

You wait beside my bed
like a bride
who no longer pretends
to enjoy or understand anything.

Portrait of My Lover as a Bungalow

Find a quiet field
and lie down.
Surround yourself with roses
and a hedge.
And then, O Lord,
let me lie beside you
and stroke you
as I would
a dead lion.

Portrait of My Lover as a Butterfly

Inch yourself, O Lord,
into a leotard,
double-check your map,
adjust your wings,
and then, O Lord, before it is too late,
make your way at once into the mountains
to live a life of weightlessness
and rigour.

Portrait of My Lover in a Car

Lean against me, Lord,
like a lover
lying in a car in a lake
and leaning out against a shoal of minnows
that makes it hard, O Lord,
for him to know
if he is merely dead
or being worshipped.

Portrait of My Lover as a Cardigan

Wrap me in your arms
like a cardigan
made of the skins
of hundreds of knitted basset hounds
wrapping themselves around a small piglet.

Portrait of My Lover as a Chicken

If only you had been
a little chicken
living quietly
in a chicken-run
nobody, O Lord,
would have to tell you
they never even loved you anyway.

Portrait of My Lover with Chocolate Biscuits

My beautiful Lord
who comes rising out of the snow
with large bejewelled hands and chocolate biscuits
tells me in my dreams, as I in yours,
it's too late now for wanting to be held.

Portrait of My Lover as a Cockroach

You kiss me
like a scratchy little cockroach
scuttling across a concrete floor
in a wedding-dress.

Portrait of My Lover in a Cot

Air, my darling, is a giant ear
that never stops
pretending it can't hear.
So cry, my darling,
from your little cot;
cry to air,
your blue, your only mamma.

Portrait of My Lover with a Crochet Hook

Look down, O Lord,
and shower me with roses
as fragrant and as chunky, Lord, as cake;
look down, my love,
and with your little crochet hook
pick the sorrow from my brain
like crab.

Portrait of My Lover as a Crocodile

I wake to find you
stretched along my thigh –
as motionless and dozy
as a crocodile
that only ever eats semolina.

Portrait of My Lover as a Crow

Understudy light,
and when it's dark
fall asleep against my brown ear.

Portrait of My Lover as a Cushion

Be fat.
Grow laps.
Relax, O Lord,
and practise
being not only boneless
but serene.
Find a quiet sofa
and just sit there
doing nothing
like a square goose
that knows the only way
to be my lover
is actually to be
a small cushion.

Portrait of My Lover as a Dead Fish

Morning,
like an ice-pink cardigan
stiff with buttons made of wind and rain,
finds you floating
upside-down, O Lord,
and much too sick to know the word for *mercy*.

Portrait of My Lover as a Distant Mountain

How faint
you have become, O Lord,
like mist
where tiny mountain goats,
alert and numberless,
follow paths
that are three-quarters air.

Portrait of My Lover as a Dog

You lie in bed and watch me like a dog
watching deer
wander round the house.

Portrait of My Lover as a Doll

Curl your hair, Lord,
simplify your brain,
and burrow down
inside my towelling dressing-gown
where dolls, O Lord,
are treated to rough kisses
as warm and thick as slices of Peru.

Portrait of My Lover as a Donkey

Imagine I'm a carnival, O Lord.
Smell the flowers.
Stroke the giant moths.
Imagine I am swaying, Lord,
and stamping.
Imagine you're a rather bony donkey.

Portrait of My Lover as a Dredger

You groan beside me, Lord,
like a dredger
that groans with the weight of a thousand rock-hard dreams.

Portrait of My Lover as a Dress

Scream
like a dress, O Lord,
an unknown girl
with crimson lips
and legs like chicken bones
sticks a pair
of kitchen scissors into.

Portrait of My Lover as an Ear

I roam the world
in search of large beige ears
that comfort and uplift
the broken-hearted.

Portrait of My Lover as an Elephant

Welcome
to my serpentine hotel
where elephants exterminate small fish
by sucking them out of the fishtanks with their trunks
and squeezing them tighter and tighter until they die
and the glittering corpses catch in their ears like tiaras
that drop to the floor
where anyone running will skid
and sink without trace down a tunnel of endless night
where elephant babies are rocking themselves to sleep
while making peculiar little gasping noises.

Portrait of My Lover as the Emperor Wu

O let me be your baby,
Velveteen:
part your robes;
let me call you Wu.

Portrait of My Lover as an Engineer

You crawl towards me like an engineer
who works all night in dangerous passages
crying out for love
in ancient languages.

Portrait of My Lover's Eyes

Shadows spread across your eyes like wax
across small lakes tall women use as skating-rinks.

Portrait of My Lover's Face

Averse to the feel
of anything warmer
than ice,
your face,
O Lord,
is tinged,
like height,
with blue.

Portrait of My Lover as a Fall of Snow

Think snow, O Lord.
Think flurries of warm snow.
Sprinkle it across the land like tinsel;
like Cabbage Whites,
the sound of pillows,
sheep;
or like, O Lord, the whites of your sad eyes
if I dried them
and chopped them
and gave them small parachutes.

Portrait of My Lover as a Fish

On certain days
when all I do is swim
I entertain
a certain large fish
by teaching it
the fishes' word for *mercy*.

Portrait of My Lover as a Flower Arrangement

You're like a sort of resident flower-arrangement –
so handsome, Lord,
so stiff,
so *in the way.*

Portrait of My Lover as My Future Husband

Quaint lands of cocktails
lie in wait
like buckets
to drown tame wives
who marry
but won't purr.

Portrait of My Lover as a Glass of Water

Slither down my throat
like mountain passes
made of liquid rock
called perfect water
born to be the only one to satisfy
my large and small and medium-sized thirsts.

Portrait of My Lover as a Goat

You act as if there's no such thing as Ovaltine,
no such thing as wanting to be held.
You act as if it's even too much bother
to hold my hand.
You should have been a goat.

Portrait of My Lover as a Goose

Geese were made to paddle in small ponds
and eat warm mash
and live on citadels.
Geese were made, my darling,
to be eaten,
by candle-light.
You should have been a goose.

Portrait of My Lover as a Great Dane

You lean against me like a large dog
that doesn't want to know
it's far from home.

Portrait of My Lover as a Gun

Your lips, O Lord,
hairless
and indifferent,
rest against my temples
like a gun.

Portrait of My Lover as a Handbag

The shape you make, O Lord,
is handbag-shaped,
with lots of inner pockets
no one visits
where bits of fluff
mill around in darkness
like bits of God
in the process of not becoming.

Portrait of My Lover as a Hen

Couldn't you become a little hen
and live inside a coop
like Marlon Brando?
Wouldn't you enjoy a little house
where nothing happens
and you can't go wrong?

Portrait of My Lover as Hildegard of Bingen

O take yourself to Bingen
and a cell
with a narrow bed
and spectacular views of the sea
and a constant supply
of uplifting musical instruments
shaped like intestines
made of beaten gold.

Portrait of My Lover as a Holy Mother

You sit beside me
like a Holy Mother
sitting alone in the back of a limousine.

Portrait of My Lover as a Hook

Please invent a special kind of hook
to comfort and uplift the broken-hearted;
and please invent a special kind of sky
to which I can be carried
by the hook.

Portrait of My Lover as a Houseboat

How sweet and heavy, Lord, you lie,
like houseboats
rocking themselves
against old banks or barges.

Portrait of My Lover as an Iridescent Whale

Take your clothes off.
Fill your car with mud.
Then ease yourself into this large suit
whose thunderous and iridescent tail
will take you straight
to where desire began.

Portrait of My Lover as a Jug

Slip your clothes off, Lord,
and be my jug
for pouring cream
from cows
late coming home.

Portrait of My Lover as a Kitchenette

I would like to be married, O Lord,
to a kitchenette
whose overstated but misleading radiance
belies the fact
it's easy to maintain.

Portrait of My Lover as My Late Father's Suit

Flannel suits
with button-holes for eyes
follow me around
like small gods
that come from somewhere cold
that smells of fish
where nobody grows
and even the beds are small.

Portrait of My Lover as a Lollipop

You wait beside me
like a lollipop
aching for the warmth
of children's tongues.

Portrait of My Lover as a Lugworm

I'd like to be a very long tunnel.
I'd like to feel your cheeks against my sides.
I'd like to take you home to where the mud
can't remember why it's got no stones.

Portrait of My Lover as a Molehill or Molehills

What you really need
is a lullaby
to tunnel down inside your ears like moles
and turn you inside-out
like male molehills
that know exactly
how to be content.

Portrait of My Lover as a Motorway

You sleep beside me
like a motorway
where flat tin lorries
lie in warm rows
praising God
for letting them be stationary.

Portrait of My Lover's Mouth

Your mouth is like a mouthful of raw liver
whose crunchy flap's too icy to be sliced.

Portrait of My Lover as a Neapolitan Mastiff

Your only dreams, O Lord,
must be of me,
my little arms
so tight around your neck
you can't remember, Lord,
if you can move.

Portrait of My Lover as a Newt

Your tongue
inside my mouth
is like a newt
beside the penis
of a small baby.

Portrait of My Lover as a Nipple

O Lord and Master,
be my little ear,
an aligned and relaxed and resilient
little brown ear,
like a little brown troglodyte, Lord,
in a little brown cave;
or anything hidden,
anything modest like that,
anything mute,
that I can lie down beside,
and whisper to,
and feel calmed by, Lord;
like the ear of a calf,
or a freckled astronomer,
or a tea-bag or herb-bag or old-fashioned lavender-bag
slipped into little pouches of downy velvet;
I would like you, Lord, to be brown
and become blind:
I would like the world to be nothing but white wool,
with me in the middle,
as nothing but white lips:
I would like you, Lord, to become,
not an ear, like I said,
but a little brown nipple.
Can you manage that?

Portrait of My Lover as a Nose-Stud

Bring your flabby body
to my nose.
Drain it.
Dry it.
Whet it.
Punch it in.

Portrait of My Lover as an Omelette

O to be an undernourished spinster
standing at a window with an omelette
and gazing out
across a cul-de-sac
that shimmers
like the days before sin.

Portrait of My Lover as a Parrot

What used to hop around me like a parrot
has stuffed itself inside me with such force
I'm left with nothing, Lord,
but lumps of parrot-meat
and little mirrors with their pointless bells.

Portrait of My Lover as a Pearl

Reduce yourself,
O Lord,
to a pearl
made of nothing
but grains of polished sand
training themselves to become perfect spheres.

Portrait of My Lover as a Pig

Pigs are made to squelch in endless fields
like muddy chocs.
You should have been a pig.

Portrait of My Lover as a Pineapple Fritter

Wild lips
are biting into fruit
that oozes juice
through cracks
in batter jackets
that scratch my tongue
and tickle my fat cheeks
in a tinkling shower
of grease-encrusted sugar.

Portrait of My Lover as a Pool

May your lap, O Lord,
become a pool
for me to float around in
upside-down –
untouchable,
myopic
and repeatedly
blessing you
for having deliquesced.

Portrait of My Lover as a Poulterer

Your mouth is like a pair of rubber boots
that trample on my hair and smell of duck.

Portrait of My Lover as a Quince

Relax, my darling,
like the pear-shaped quince
that hangs in trees
not thinking about pears.

Portrait of My Lover as Real Snow

Real snow is beautiful
and murderous
and never sleeps
and never feels cold
and falls, O Lord,
we tell ourselves,
from Paradise,
to settle,
like white lips,
on small homes.

Portrait of My Lover as a Root

All you know is what a root knows
that only knows the language of perversity
and how to cling
and how to fear light.

Portrait of My Lover as a Saint

To qualify yourself as my lover
you need to go and get yourself beatified
then try again –
floating on a cloudlet,
and carrying a harp
or a lute.

Portrait of My Lover as a Saucepan

Saucepans spend the day being useful
and spend the night alone and upsidedown
dreaming of white coffee and pink fingers
without the need of needing to be loved.

Portrait of My Lover as My Second Husband

Smiles, Lord,
like fish the size of horses
swimming in and out of upstairs windows,
fail to make sense of who we are
standing here in our best clothes.

Portrait of My Lover as a Seraph

Stand, O Lord,
above my precipice,
then, leaning forward, beg the sky for wings.

Portrait of My Lover as My Servant

You prop yourself against me
like the servant
the poor demented empress
plied with lollipops
she kept inside her sleeves
like pet birds
ever since the fatal day
she murdered him.

Portrait of My Lover as a Shepherd

I wish you, Lord, a little hut on wheels;
I wish you snow;
I wish you rolling downs;
I wish you, Lord, a little snow-proof lover
for teaching how to graze
and how to bleat.

Portrait of My Lover as a Ship

I fear for you, O Lord.
The way you move.
As if you can't.
Like a great ship.

Portrait of My Lover as a Shrimp

You huddle on my sofa
like a shrimp
none of whose soft knees
can bear weight.

Portrait of My Lover's Skull

Whatever it is that makes the mothers of babies
know at once
when something's not quite right
makes me know you've got a little living-room
tucked inside your skull
where someone's ironing.

Portrait of My Lover as a Spoon

When you're next in Argentina, Lord,
can you get some DULCE DE LECHE for me?
To be gobbled up straight from the tin
with my little spoon
in my big dark house
where I'm pacing about, O Lord,
craving something sweet,
because sweetness and thickness
was where I went wrong, O Lord,
and you're more like ice
and all I need now is a plastic spoon for my jelly,
O all I need now is a white, moulded spoon
to hold in my hand
as I wait for my white milk jelly.
(You'll know it, O Lord, by the photograph of the cow
stretching around the tin like a white dachshund.)

Portrait of My Lover as a Strange Animal

Don't ask me why
but soon I started feeding it,
on caterpillars, chocolate drops, soft fruit –
anything as long as it was small.
Its mouth was as small and tight as a wedding-ring.
On moonlit nights it liked to watch the stars
and lean against me
like a giant jelly.
Then came the night I thought I heard it speak.
It said my name!
O Lord, it sounded beautiful!...
But of course by then I was out of my mind with exhaustion.
I had sunk to my knees in the sand I was so exhausted.
And the sacks I had carried contained only roots.
And as for my name –
it was only the sound of its gums
crunching the body
of its final wren.

Portrait of My Lover as a Sugar Mouse

Sugar mice are pink and white like you,
like juicy shrimp,
sweet mummified flamingoes;
like almonds dipped in tails,
crunchy thumbs;
sugared rose-buds,
frosted collies' noses;
baby voles in overcoats
too young,
too frivolous,
to know the word farewell;
like roast potatoes,
chopped and crystallised,
the hands of clocks
delighted to be free;
whittled, shrink-wrapped
hunch-backed sugar tongues:
I'd rather suck a nest of sugar mice
than you, O Lord.
So see what you can do.

Portrait of My Lover as a Suitcase

I want to live alone
with my suitcase,
a length of ribbon
and a tiny key –
as tiny
as the visions of eternity
brought to us
by faultless counter-tenors.

Portrait of My Lover as a Swan

A frozen lake
encrusted with dead swans
is not as stiff
as how I lie with you.

Portrait of My Lover as a Swimming-Pool

Be turquoise, Lord
and lean
and horizontal
and summon divers
in the dead of night
to sacrifice themselves
to needing air
and climbing silence
to inhabit height.

Portrait of My Lover as a Teapot

I'd like to have a lover like a teapot
that regularly plays the violin
with all the sweet indifference of dreams
to sleepy women in remote hotels.

Portrait of My Lover as a Tutu

Imagine you're as crunchy as white lettuces.
Imagine you're obsessed by skin-tight tights.
Imagine days investigating swanneries.
Imagine nights impersonating flight.
Imagine being mine,
and solving everything
by simply twirling round and being white.

Portrait of My Lover as an Upmarket Snack

Take the car
and go to Mexico
and sit in vats of honey
like a root
and when you're dead
I'll lay you out on tablecloths
and sell you to fat tourists
as rare fruit.

Portrait of My Lover as a Vale

Imagine you're a vale full of stones.
Imagine I can flood you with my tears.
Imagine I can swim across quite easily
to somewhere *made of algebra and fire.*

Portrait of My Lover as a Viburnum

You stand there looking bored
like a viburnum
pining for a road-side garden centre.

Portrait of My Lover as a Wardrobe

You watch me
like a wardrobe
in a sick-room
watching writhing women
without interest.

Portrait of My Lover as a Washing-Machine

Get white;
eat sheets;
and with your rubber throat
roar, O Lord,
for daring to be mine.

Portrait of My Lover with a Water Beetle

The more you weep
the more warm ponds there are
for me to whizz around in
like a water-beetle,
glinting meanly
like a hot bazaar.

Portrait of My Lover as a Wheelbarrow

I'll need a little shed to keep you in;
I'll need a coat;
I'll need a long night;
and then, O Lord,
with you to hold my hand,
I'll crawl into my little shed
and yowl.

Portrait of My Lover as a Wind-Sock

O to be the mistress of a wind-sock
in which the wandering wind
can rest its foot;
to billow in the sun
like bone-dry washing
the size and shape of an airborne
bungalow.

Portrait of My Lover as My Ex-Lover

I have fallen in love with the Gobi Desert, O Lord.
I have fallen in love with arms in the shape of hair.
I have fallen in love with lips like bible lands.
I have fallen in love, O Lord.
Wish me well.

Portrait of My Lover as a Yellow Camper Van

May you be undaunted and bright yellow,
may you hit the open road, O Lord;
may you have warm animals inside you
and strings of tinkly bells
dangling from you.

Portrait of My Lover as a Zebra

Grow a tail,
elongate your ears
and tiptoe through my garden
as a zebra –
a zebra who will take me out for rides
over the heath
to the sandman's private forest
where just to smell the pine-trees is enough,
to be dressed in a dress
embroidered with wild moths
the bedrooms of the married
are much too airless for;
where the sandy zebras' polished hooves on the pine-cones
crack like sound of abbots
cracking the spines of books
as gold and neat, my love,
as precious spectacles;
where the rabbits are striped
and the zebra's a friend of mine
and the eyes of the cats
are the colour of Vegemite jars:
O grant me, Lord, one night
beside a zebra,
one perfect sandy night
beside a zebra
that lets me rest my head against its neck.